TV COOKS

Mary Berry

COOKS

Puddings
&
Desserts

Photographs by Philip Webb

BBC BOOKS

Published by BBC Books,
an imprint of BBC Consumer Publishing.
BBC Worldwide Limited, Woodlands,
80 Wood Lane, London W12 0TT.

The recipes in this book first appeared in:
Glorious puds
© Mary Berry 1980
Mary Berry's Quick & Easy Cakes
© Mary Berry 1993
Mary Berry's Ultimate Cake Book
© Mary Berry 1994

This edition first published 1997
© Mary Berry 1997
The moral right of the author
has been asserted

ISBN 0 563 38347 X

Edited by Pam Mallender
Designed by DW Design
Photographs by Philip Webb
Styling by Helen Payne
Home Economist Jane Stevenson
Author photograph by Clay Perry

Set in New Caledonia and Helvetica
Printed and bound in France by Imprimerie Pollina s.a.
Colour origination by Radstock Reproduction Ltd,
Midsomer Norton
Cover printed in France by Imprimerie Pollina s.a.

Cover: Hazelnut Meringue Cake.
Frontispiece: Chocolate Roulade.

CONTENTS

Recipe Notes and Handy Conversion Tables	**4**
Introduction by Mary Berry	**5**
Equipment Glossary	**6**
Equipment	**8**
Meringues	**10**
Pies & Tarts	**18**
No-cook Desserts	**29**
Soufflés	**37**
Favourite Hot Puds	**41**
Chilled Desserts	**46**
Chocolate Desserts	**57**
Ice Creams	**62**
Index	**64**

RECIPE NOTES

Eggs are size 3, unless otherwise stated. If your kitchen is warm, keep the eggs in the fridge, but allow them to come to room temperature before using. While the proven risks of healthy people becoming ill from eating fresh raw eggs is minimal, pregnant women, the sick, the elderly and the very young should not do so just in case.

Spoon measurements are level. Always use proper measuring spoons:
1 teaspoon = 5ml and 1 tablespoon = 15ml.
Never mix metric and imperial measures in one recipe. Stick to one or the other.

HANDY CONVERSION TABLES

Weight		Volume		Linear	
15g	½oz	30ml	1fl oz	5mm	¼in
25g	1oz	50ml	2fl oz	10mm/1cm	½in
40g	1½oz	100ml	3½fl oz	2cm	¾in
55g	2oz	125ml	4fl oz	2.5cm	1in
85g	3oz	150ml	5fl oz (¼ pint)	5cm	2in
115g	4oz	175ml	6fl oz	7.5cm	3in
140g	5oz	200ml	7fl oz (⅓ pint)	10cm	4in
175g	6oz	225ml	8fl oz	13cm	5in
200g	7oz	250ml	9fl oz	15cm	6in
225g	8oz	300ml	10fl oz (½ pint)	18cm	7in
250g	9oz	350ml	12fl oz	20cm	8in
280g	10oz	400ml	14fl oz	23cm	9in
350g	12oz	425ml	15fl oz (¾ pint)	25cm	10in
375g	13oz	450ml	16fl oz	28cm	11in
400g	14oz	500ml	18fl oz	30cm	12in
425g	15oz	600ml	20fl oz (1 pint)		
450g	1lb	700ml	1¼ pints	**Oven temperatures**	
550g	1¼lb	850ml	1½ pints	225F 110C GAS ¼	
750g	1lb 10oz	1 litre	1¾ pints	250F 120C GAS ½	
900g	2lb	1.2 litres	2 pints	275F 140C GAS 1	
1kg	2¼lb	1.3 litres	2¼ pints	300F 150C GAS 2	
1.3kg	3lb	1.4 litres	2½ pints	325F 160C GAS 3	
1.8kg	4lb	1.7 litres	3 pints	350F 180C GAS 4	
2.25kg	5lb	2 litres	3½ pints	375F 190C GAS 5	
		2.5 litres	4½ pints	400F 200C GAS 6	
				425F 220C GAS 7	
				450F 230C GAS 8	
				475F 240C GAS 9	

✳ **Suitable for freezing**

The recipes in this little book are all my real favourites, tried and tested at home for family occasions and ideal for entertaining too.

I have included lots of shortcuts here, for example I have used ready-made flan cases, bought pastry and canned fruits. I have also tried to make use of the wide variety of fresh fruits now easily available from supermarkets all the year round.

The joy of many of these desserts is that they can be made a day or so ahead or indeed frozen. I have given details about freezing throughout the book along with nutritional information and fat content for those of you who are watching your waistlines.

Of course I've included a chocolate cake, this time Death by Chocolate Cake. This rich but irresistable dessert is even better with a good blob of cream. There are two roulades, a chocolate one and a meringue one which can be on the table in half an hour. No puddings book would be complete without the old-fashioned favourites so I have simple recipes for classics like Crème Caramel, Crème Brûlée, Tarte Tatin and little Treacle Sponges, wonderful on cold days.

One of the great things about making puddings and desserts for entertaining is that you can do them well in advance and be relaxed to receive your guests. You feel the job's done and you can enjoy the party.

I do hope you and your family and friends will enjoy these tempting desserts as much as mine do.

Mary Berry.

EQUIPMENT

Baking papers
I usually use greaseproof paper for lining cake tins which don't have loose bottoms. It should be of good quality, and it is available in sheets or rolls.

Non-stick baking paper: this is sometimes called parchment and for me is a must for things containing a high proportion of sugar, such as meringues.

Lift-off paper: this is a reusable type of graphite paper. It can be used to line baking trays, roasting tins or cake tins, then simply wiped over and stored, ready for use again. It withstands domestic oven temperatures, and the manufacturers claim it can last, with regular domestic use, for more than two years.

Plastic film: this is handy for lining tins for some no-cook desserts, especially those which are fruit-based. It is also useful when using metal tins. Leave flaps or tails at the side, so that the cake can be eased out in one piece.

Baking sheets
At least three baking sheets are essential. I like these to be flat, or perhaps with a slight turn-up at one end. They should be rigid and heavy – and the right size for your oven!

Bowls
I like to have a selection of these, from large down to the very smallest, preferably made of oven glass, which will fit one inside the other. This makes for economical storage. They should have rounded bottoms so that you can get to every bit of the mixture with your whisk, spoon or spatula.

Cake tins
Good quality, strong, solid cake tins are worth the initial investment and will last you a lifetime. Cheap cake tins are likely to be very thin, may warp with use and do not conduct heat evenly.

If you do not have the size of tin specified, then choose a cake tin which is slightly larger and test the cake 5-10 minutes earlier, as the shallower cake will take less time to cook.

Non-stick: these are easy to clean, but it is wise to follow the recipe instructions for greasing and lining, and not to rely solely on the tin's non-stick properties. Choose black-lined tins, if possible, as these conduct heat better.

Loose-bottomed: these are excellent but avoid the ones with thick, insulated bases as they stop the cake cooking evenly in modern cookers. They're designed to stop the cake burning on the bottom, but they also slow the cooking down.

Sandwich tins: these should preferably be non-stick and are best with loose bases. The most used sizes are 18, 20 and 23cm/7/8/9in round.

Flan tins: if you do a lot of baking, get both deep and shallow. These, too, are best with loose bottoms.

Bun or patty tins: these can be fluted or plain with 6, 12 or 24 containers.

Food mixers and food processors
Electric hand-held mixers usually just have attachments to whip cream or egg whites, but some have attachments for mixing and creaming.

Food processors have become extremely popular and they are very time saving. But you must be very careful not to overmix a mixture. Use the pulse button where available to give you more control.

Knives
Palette knives are indispensable both to spread and smooth mixtures, and for loosening items from the sides of tins before turning out. Keen cooks need three sizes.

You will also need a long, sharp serrated knife to cut a cake cleanly into horizontal layers.

Measuring spoons and jugs

A set of measuring spoons, preferably plastic, is vital for tablespoon and teaspoon measurements. All the amounts given in the recipes are for level spoonfuls unless otherwise stated. For liquids, use a jug that is see-through, heatproof and shows both metric and imperial measures.

Ovens

Regrettably, no two ovens are the same whether they are gas, electric or fan-assisted. All the recipes in this book were tested in a conventional oven. Particular care is needed with the timing of fan ovens as they can all too quickly dry out baked items by overcooking. Most fan oven manufacturers recommend lowering the specified temperature by 10C, but you may find lowering by 20C is more successful. Make a note beside each recipe of the exact cooking time in your oven. If the time varies enormously, then check your oven with an oven thermometer. Unless specified otherwise, cook items in the centre of the oven and check about three-quarters of the way through the cooking time to see if they are done.

Pastry essentials

A long wooden rolling pin with no handles is best. I like to use a pastry brush which is more like a paintbrush to glaze pastry, or brush melted fat over a tin.

Piping bags

These should be made of easily washable material such as nylon. Plastic and polythene bags are available, too. Alternatively, you could slot one small plastic bag inside another, then snip off the corners at one side.

Sieves

Strong, well-made sieves are best. They come in a variety of sizes and can be put in the dishwasher. (Old wire can come out of wire sieves, and they can more easily become misshapen.) It's vital to have a nylon sieve for fruit, as fruits such as raspberries react with metal.

Spatulas

I now always use a rubber, bendy spatula. It's most useful for getting all of a mixture off the sides of a bowl into the tin. It must never be put in the dishwasher or in boiling liquid, or stored by a warm oven as the rubber quickly perishes with heat.

Spoons

One wooden spoon, with a rounded bottom (no need for a hole) to get into the bends of bowls is a real asset. A wooden spoon or spatula with a flat, cut-off end can be used in a pan. A large metal spoon is useful for mixing egg whites into a mixture, as its slimmer edges flatten the egg foam much less than a wooden spoon.

Whisks

I like to use balloon whisks in two sizes, a larger one for blending eggs together, and a small spiral one for small amounts of mixture – easier in many cases than using an electrical gadget, and they can get into a corner or bend of a bowl.

Wire racks

At least two of these are vital for cooling items once they have been baked; round ones are available which look attractive hung on the wall, but large rectangular ones are better. Or you can use the rack from your grill pan.

1 Baking sheet

2 Wire cooling racks

3 Wooden spoons

4 Rolling pin

5 Balloon whisks

6 Loose-bottomed cake tin

7 Spring-release tin

8 Loaf tin

9 Baking beans

10 Electric hand whisk

11 Wire sieves

12 Measuring spoons

13 Soufflé dish

14 Measuring jug

15 Pastry brush

16 Non-stick baking parchment

17 Scales

18 Sandwich tin

19 Nylon sieve

20 Palette knife

21 Flan tin

22 Swiss roll tin

23 Bun tin

24 Piping bag

25 Fluted cutters

26 Nozzles

27 Pie dish

28 Glass mixing bowl

Meringues

RASPBERRY MERINGUE ROULADE ❋

This is rather an unusual idea, which makes a generous roulade that is an excellent for a party.

Makes 8–10 slices

5 egg whites, at room temperature
280g/10oz caster sugar
55g/2oz flaked almonds
FOR THE FILLING
300ml/½ pint whipping cream
350g/12oz fresh raspberries

1 Preheat the oven to 425F/220C/Gas 7. Line a 33x23cm/13x9in Swiss roll tin with greased non-stick baking paper.

2 Whisk the egg whites with an electric whisk on full speed until very stiff. Still at full speed, gradually add the sugar, a teaspoon at a time, whisking well between each addition. Whisk until very, very stiff and all the sugar has been incorporated. (This will take about 8–10 minutes.)

3 Spread the meringue mixture into the tin and sprinkle with the almonds. Place the tin near the top of the oven and bake for about 12 minutes until pale golden. Then, lower the oven temperature to 325F/160C/Gas 3 and bake the roulade for a further 15 minutes until firm to the touch.

4 Remove the meringue from the oven and turn, almond side down, on to a sheet of non-stick baking paper. Remove the paper from the base of the cooked meringue and leave to cool for 10 minutes.

5 Meanwhile, make the filling. Whisk the cream until it stands in stiff peaks, and gently mix in the raspberries. Spread the raspberries and cream evenly over the meringue. Start to roll from the long end fairly tightly until rolled up. Wrap in non-stick baking paper and chill before serving.

Nutrition notes per serving for eight: *399 calories, Protein 6g, Carbohydrate 40g, Fat 25g, Saturated fat 11g, Fibre 2g, Added sugar 37g, Salt 0.07g.*

❋ *This freezes extremely well. Simply wrap in foil and allow about 8 hours to defrost before serving. If you are making the roulade specifically for freezing and are using frozen raspberries, don't bother to defrost them, just add to the cream. Freeze the whole cake, then defrost when required.*

TIP

Store leftover egg yolks in the fridge in a small container. Pour a tablespoon of cold water over the top, then cover with plastic film. Use within 1 week. They are ideal to enrich sauces, or add to scrambled egg and omelette mixtures. You could also use them in the recipe for Crème brûlée (page 49).

PAVLOVA ⊛

Don't worry about cracks on the top – this is all part of the charm.

Serves 8

4 egg whites, at room temperature

225g/8oz caster sugar

1½ tsp cornflour

1½ tsp white wine vinegar

FOR THE FILLING

350g/12oz fresh fruits, such as blueberries, kiwi fruit and raspberries

425ml/¾ pint whipping cream, whipped

1   Preheat the oven to 325F/160C/Gas 3. Lay a sheet of non-stick baking paper on a baking sheet and mark out a 23–25cm/9–10in circle.

2   Whisk the egg whites with an electric mixer on full speed until stiff. Still at full speed, gradually add the sugar, a teaspoon at a time, whisking well between each addition. Blend the cornflour and wine vinegar together and whisk into the meringue. Spread the meringue out to cover the circle on the baking sheet, building up the sides so that they are higher than the middle.

3   Place in the oven, then immediately reduce the temperature to 300F/150C/Gas 2. Bake for about 1–1¼ hours until firm to the touch and pale beige. Turn off the oven and leave the Pavlova in the oven until cold. Remove from the baking sheet, fill with cream and fruit. Chill for 1 hour before serving.

Nutrition notes per serving: *336 calories, Protein 3g, Carbohydrate 36g, Fat 21g, Saturated fat 13g, Fibre 1g, Added sugar 30g, Salt 0.14g.*

⊛ *Open freeze, unfilled, until solid. As it is likely to be brittle, slip into a rigid plastic box to protect it. Defrost for about 8 hours at a cool room temperature.*

SPEEDY BAKED ALASKA ⊛

Impressive to serve but surprisingly easy to make. This is a great favourite with children.

Serves 6–8

18cm/7in sponge flan case

420g can mandarin oranges in light syrup, drained and syrup reserved or other canned fruit

600ml/1 pint tub good quality vanilla ice cream, softened in the fridge

sifted icing sugar, for dusting

FOR THE MERINGUE TOPPING

2 egg whites, at room temperature

115g/4oz caster sugar

few flaked almonds

1   Preheat the oven to 450F/230C/Gas 8. Place the flan case in a shallow freezer and ovenproof dish and arrange mandarin oranges over the base.

2   Sprinkle one tablespoon of reserved syrup over the fruit. Invert the ice cream on to the mandarin oranges. Place in the freezer.

3   Using an electric mixer, whisk the egg whites at full speed until they stand in soft peaks. Still whisking at full speed, gradually add the sugar, a teaspoon at a time, whisking well between each addition and keeping the mixture stiff.

4   Spoon the meringue all over the sponge and ice cream, making sure you enclose both completely. Swirl the meringue and sprinkle with almonds.

5   Bake immediately for 3–4 minutes or until well browned. Dust with icing sugar.

Nutrition notes per serving for six: *416 calories, Protein 9g, Carbohydrate 71g, Fat 13g, Saturated fat 7g, Fibre 1g, Added sugar 52g, Salt 0.31g.*

⊛ *Open freeze the Alaska, before baking, until solid. Carefully cover or place in a rigid plastic box to protect it. Defrost for 30 minutes before baking.*

COFFEE AND BANANA VACHERIN ✸

If you are in a hurry you could just spread the meringue rather than making spirals.

4 egg whites, at room temperature

115g/4oz caster sugar

115g/4oz light muscovado sugar

FOR THE FILLING

300ml/½ pint double cream

1 tsp instant coffee

2 slightly under-ripe bananas

TO FINISH

sifted icing sugar, for dusting

150ml/¼ pint double cream, whipped

1 Preheat the oven to 275F/140C/Gas 1. Line two baking sheets with non-stick baking paper and mark each one with a 20cm/8in circle.

2 Place the egg whites in a large bowl and whisk on high speed with an electric whisk until stiff. Add the sugar, a teaspoon at a time, whisking well at high speed after each addition, until all the sugar has been added.

3 Spoon the meringue mixture into a large nylon piping bag fitted with a 1cm/½in plain nozzle. Starting at the centre of the drawn circles, pipe the meringue into two circles on the baking sheets in a spiral pattern.

4 Bake for about 1–1¼ hours or until the meringues are crisp, dry and lightly coloured. Allow to cool in the oven, then peel off the baking paper.

5 Make the filling: whip the cream until it holds its shape, then flavour with the coffee dissolved in a little water. Slice the bananas thinly and fold into the cream making sure they are well coated to prevent discolouration. Spread over one meringue circle, then place the other circle on top. Dust lightly with icing sugar and decorate with rosettes of whipped cream. Leave 3 hours before serving.

Nutrition notes per serving: *531 calories, Protein 4g, Carbohydrate 51g, Fat 36g, Saturated fat 23g, Fibre trace, Added sugar 41g, Salt 0.18g.*

✸ *Open freeze the meringue circles until solid. As they are likely to be brittle, slip them into a rigid plastic box to protect them. Allow plenty of time for them to defrost – about 8 hours at a cool room temperature, then fill with the bananas and cream and decorate.*

You can make the meringue circles up to 2 weeks in advance. Store carefully in polythene bags in an airtight tin.

HAZELNUT MERINGUE CAKE ✱

This has become a classic favourite, the raspberries and hazelnuts being a particularly good combination. It's delicous served with a raspberry coulis (optional). Fill the meringue about three hours before serving; it will then cut into portions without splintering. Walnuts can be used in place of the hazelnuts in the meringue. Choose a fruit to complement them, such as strawberries or ripe peaches in season.

Serves 6

140g/5oz shelled hazelnuts

4 egg whites, at room temperature

250g/9oz caster sugar

few drops vanilla essence

½ tsp white wine vinegar

sifted icing sugar, for dusting

FOR THE RASPBERRY COULIS

225g/8oz raspberries

4 tbsp sifted icing sugar

FOR THE FILLING

300ml/½ pint whipping cream

225g/8oz raspberries

1 Preheat the oven to 325F/160C/Gas 3. Lightly brush two 20cm/8in sandwich tins with oil and line the base and sides with non-stick baking parchment (See Tip).

2 Place the hazelnuts on a baking tray and place in the oven for about 10 minutes, then tip on to a clean tea towel and rub well together to remove the skins. (Some stubborn ones may need to go back into the oven but don't worry about getting every last bit of skin off, it's not necessary.) Place the nuts in a food processor or blender and grind until still chunky.

3 Whisk the egg whites on maximum speed with an electric whisk until stiff. Add the sugar, a teaspoon at a time, and continue whisking, still at top speed, until the mixture is very stiff, stands in peaks, and all the sugar has been added. Whisk in the vanilla essence and wine vinegar, then fold in the nuts. Divide the mixture between the tins and smooth the top with a palette knife.

4 Bake for 45 minutes–1 hour. The top of the meringues will be crisp and the insides soft like a marshmallow. Turn out of the tins, remove the baking paper and allow to cool on a wire rack.

5 Make the raspberry coulis: place the raspberries in a food processor and blend until they form a purée, then push the purée through a nylon sieve into a bowl to remove the seeds. Gradually whisk in the icing sugar.

6 Whisk the cream until thick and use two-thirds to fill the meringue along with the raspberries. Dust the meringue with icing sugar and use remaining cream to pipe rosettes on top. Leave for 3 hours and serve with the raspberry coulis.

Nutrition notes per serving: *562calories, Protein 7g, Carbohydrate 60g, Fat 35g, Saturated fat 13g, Fibre 2g, Added sugar 55g, Salt 0.16g.*

✱ *Open freeze the filled, undecorated, meringue until solid. As it is likely to be brittle, slip it into a rigid plastic box to protect it. Allow about 8 hours at a cool room temperature for it to defrost. Dust with icing sugar and pipe on the rosettes of cream just before serving. Freeze the coulis in a freezer bag or small plastic container. Defrost before serving.*

TIP

If you don't have sandwich tins, cook the meringue on two flat baking sheets. Spread it into two circles. It won't look quite so neat, but it will taste the same!

Pies & Tarts

LEMON CREAM FRUIT TARTS

These lovely little shortbread cases can actually be filled with anything you like – a good way of spinning out a small amount of fruit, like the first strawberries, for instance. They're quite crumbly to eat. If time is limited use bought shortcrust pastry instead of shortbread.

Makes about 10 tarts

FOR THE SHORTBREAD

115g/4oz butter, softened

55g/2oz caster sugar

55g/2oz semolina

1 egg yolk

115g/4oz plain flour

FOR THE FILLING

about 3 tbsp good lemon curd

150ml/¼ pint double cream, whipped

fresh hulled and sliced strawberries

1 Make the shortbread: soften the butter in a bowl, add the sugar, semolina, egg yolk and flour and work together to form a smooth dough. Wrap in plastic film and chill the dough in the fridge for about 15 minutes.

2 Preheat the oven to 300F/150C/Gas 2. On a lightly floured work surface, roll out the shortbread to just under 5mm/¼in thick. Cut out circles using a 7.5cm/3in fluted cutter, then ease the circles into a bun-tin tray. Prick the bases well.

3 Bake for about 20–25 minutes or until firm and golden. Leave the shortbread in the tins to harden slightly, then ease out of the tins and leave to cool completely on a wire rack.

4 Make the filling: mix together the lemon curd and the whipped cream. Just before serving, spoon a little of the filling into each shortbread case and top with sliced strawberries. Once the shortbread cases are filled, they go soft very quickly, so serve and eat straightaway.

Nutrition notes per serving: *257 calories, Protein 3g, Carbohydrate 22g, Fat 18g, Saturated fat 11g, Fibre 1g, Added sugar 8g, Salt 0.28g.*

❋ *The shortbread cases can be made ahead or frozen in a rigid plastic box to prevent them from breaking. Defrost at room temperature, then fill.*

TIP

For a really good shortbread it is essential to use butter, not margarine. Cornflour or ground rice can replace the semolina. Shortbread, traditionally eaten at Christmas and New Year, can be decoratively shaped in wooden or earthernware moulds and you can use the above recipe. Lightly flour the mould, press the shortbread dough into the patterned depression, level with a rolling pin, then turn out on to a baking tray, patterned side up and chill until firm. Bake in an oven preheated to 325F/160C/Gas 3 for 35 minutes or until a very pale golden brown. Alternatively, press the dough out into a greased 18cm/7in loose-bottomed sandwich tin, bake as before, then mark into eight wedges. Cool in the tin and dust with caster sugar.

FILO APPLE STRUDELS ✪

Try to find the shorter packets of filo pastry, then you won't need to trim the pastry to size. Any filo not used will store in the fridge for two days, or wrap it carefully, freeze and use within one month.

Serves 8

8 x 18x33cm/7x13in sheets filo pastry

115g/4oz butter, melted

FOR THE FILLING

350g/12oz prepared peeled, cored and roughly chopped cooking apples

juice of ½ lemon

85g/3oz demerara sugar

25g/1oz fresh brown breadcrumbs

55g/2oz sultanas

1 tsp ground cinnamon

FOR THE TOPPING

2 tbsp caster sugar

sifted icing sugar, for dusting

1 Preheat the oven to 400F/200C/Gas 6. Lightly grease two baking sheets. Make the filling: in a bowl, mix together the apples, lemon juice, sugar, breadcrumbs, sultanas and cinnamon.

2 Unfold one sheet of filo pastry and brush liberally with melted butter. Spoon one-eighth of the apple mixture to cover the middle third of the longest edge of the pastry, leaving a small border. Fold in this border, then bring the two short sides over the apple to cover. Roll the filled pastry over and over to form a neat strudel. Place on a baking sheet, then repeat the process with the remaining pastry sheets and filling.

3 Brush the strudels with melted butter, then bake for 15–20 minutes or until golden and crisp.

4 Meanwhile, make the topping: place the caster sugar in a small pan with two tablespoons of water. Heat gently until all the sugar has dissolved. Boil, without stirring, until a syrupy, coating consistency. Spoon the syrup over the warm strudels and dust with icing sugar, to serve.

Nutrition notes per serving: *277 calories, Protein 2g, Carbohydrate 41g, Fat 13g, Saturated fat 8g, Fibre 1g, Added sugar 16g, Salt 0.90g.*

✪ *These strudels can be frozen cooked or uncooked. Place in a rigid plastic box or polythene bags. You can then take out the number you require leaving the remainder in the freezer. Bake from frozen allowing a few minutes extra cooking time, or defrost and warm through, spoon over the syrup and dust with icing sugar.*

TIP

Filo is very thin Greek pastry made with flour, water and egg, but it does not contain much fat. It cooks in crisp, separate layers and can also be used with savoury fillings. Keep the pastry covered with a damp tea towel or plastic film after removing from the packet, otherwise it will dry out rapidly and break into a thousand pieces.

MISSISSIPPI MUD PIE

The origin of this pie is rather vague but it has become a very popular dessert in cafés and bistros. Like many American recipes it is rich, so serve in small slices. You may like to pipe the whipped cream on top of the pie for special occasions. To fill a piping bag, stand the bag and nozzle point down in a jug, then fold the top edges of the bag over the top of the jug. That way it is much easier to spoon the cream or icing into the bag without getting it all over yourself!

Serves 12

FOR THE BASE

115g/4oz digestive biscuits

55g/2oz butter, melted

25g/1oz demerara sugar

FOR THE FILLING

400g/14oz plain chocolate, broken into pieces (See Tip)

225g/8oz butter

2 tbsp instant coffee

300ml/½ pint single cream

350g/12oz light muscovado sugar

6 eggs

TO DECORATE

150ml/¼ pint whipping cream, whipped

1 Preheat the oven to 375F/190C/Gas 5. Lightly grease a 20cm/8in loose-bottomed cake tin or spring-release tin.

2 Make the base: crush the biscuits. Either place in a food processor and process until fine, or place in a plastic bag and crush with a rolling pin. Mix together with the melted butter and the sugar and spoon into the tin. Level the mixture out evenly, using the back of a metal spoon.

3 Make the filling: place the chocolate, butter, coffee and two tablespoons of boiling water in a large pan and heat gently until the butter and chocolate have melted. Remove from the heat, then beat in the cream, sugar and eggs. Pour on to the biscuit crust.

4 Bake for 1¼ hours, covering after 30 minutes to prevent over-browning, or until the filling is set. Allow to cool before removing from the tin, then decorate the top with the whipped cream. Serve chilled.

Nutrition notes per serving: *650 calories, Protein 7g, Carbohydrate 62g, Fat 43g, Saturated fat 26g, Fibre trace, Added sugar 54g, Salt 0.74g.*

TIP

The quality of chocolate varies considerably; to be called chocolate, it must have a minimum of 34 per cent cocoa butter. The finest quality block chocolate always contains a high proportion of cocoa butter, on average 35 per cent but sometimes as much as 50 per cent. The more cocoa butter it contains, the softer and creamier it will be; the less it contains, the harder and more brittle it is. The more bitter the chocolate, the more chocolate flavour it has. Plain chocolate, also called semi-sweet or bittersweet chocolate, has a rich, strong flavour, but contains enough sugar to make it palatable to eat alone. It is the chocolate most usually used in baking. There is no need to buy expensive dessert chocolates unless specified in a recipe.

TARTE TATIN

This is a classic 'upside-down' French tart. Serve warm with cream, crème fraîche or yogurt. Or try it with the Basic special ice cream (page 62).

Serves 6

FOR THE PASTRY

115g/4oz self-raising flour

55g/2oz butter, cubed

1 tbsp icing sugar, sifted

1 egg yolk

FOR THE TOPPING

85g/3oz butter

85g/3oz demerara sugar

900g/2lb Cox's dessert apples or similar (See Tip)

finely grated rind and juice of 1 lemon

2 tbsp demerara sugar (optional)

1   Make the pastry: place the flour, butter and icing sugar in a bowl. Rub in the butter until the mixture resembles fine breadcrumbs. Alternatively, make the pastry in a food processor. Add the egg yolk and enough cold water (a scant tablespoon) to bring the mixture together to a firm but not sticky dough. Knead lightly, wrap in plastic film and chill for 30 minutes.

2   Preheat the oven to 400F/200C/Gas 6. Make the topping: place the butter and sugar in a small pan and heat gently until both have melted. Pour into the base of a 23cm/9in sandwich tin.

3   Peel, core and thinly slice the apples and sprinkle over the lemon juice and rind. Arrange a single layer of the best apples in a circular pattern over the sugar and butter. Cover with the remaining apple slices.

4   Roll out the pastry on a lightly floured work surface and use to cover the apples. Bake for 20 minutes or until the pastry is crisp and golden brown. (When cooked, the pastry will have shrunk a little.)

5   Tip the juices from the tin into a small pan. Turn the tart out on to a plate with the pastry on the bottom. Boil the juices to reduce to a syrupy caramel and pour over the apples. If there is very little juice – the amount will depend on the apples – add two tablespoons of demerara sugar, dissolve in the pan with the juices and cook until syrupy.

Nutrition notes per serving: *400 calories, Protein 3g, Carbohydrate 54g, Fat 20g, Saturated fat 12g, Fibre 4g, Added sugar 23g, Salt 0.64g.*

TIP

Eating or dessert apples are used for this dessert because they retain their shape when cooked. Cooking apples, on the other hand, soften quickly and become pulpy. Cox's are available from October through to March and April. They are green and orange-red in colour with crisp, sweet, juicy and full-flavoured flesh.

LEMON MERINGUE PIE

This is a real family favourite and perfect for Sunday lunch. There's quite a lot of washing up when making it, but the recipe itself isn't too complicated. To save time, you can use a bought 23cm/9in bought pastry case. If using, add the extra egg yolk to the lemon filling.

Serves 6

FOR THE PASTRY

175g/6oz plain flour

15g/½oz icing sugar

85g/3oz butter, cubed

1 egg yolk

FOR THE FILLING

finely grated rind and juice of 2 large lemons

40g/1½oz cornflour

2 egg yolks

85g/3oz caster sugar

FOR THE MERINGUE

3 egg whites

125g/4½oz caster sugar

1 Make the pastry: place the flour and sugar in a bowl, then rub in the butter until the mixture resembles fine breadcrumbs. Add the egg yolk and about one tablespoon of cold water and work to a firm dough. This could be made in a food processor. Wrap in plastic film and leave to rest in the fridge for 30 minutes.

2 Preheat the oven to 400F/200C/Gas 6. Roll out the pastry on a lightly floured work surface and use to line a 23cm/9in loose-bottomed, fluted flan tin. Prick the pastry all over with a fork, line with greaseproof paper and fill with baking beans. Bake for 15 minutes or until the pastry is pale golden. Remove the paper and beans and bake the pastry for a further 5 minutes to allow the pastry to dry out completely.

3 Lower the oven temperature to 300F/150C/Gas 2. Make the filling: mix together the grated rind, lemon juice and cornflour in a bowl. Bring 300ml/½ pint of water to the boil, then stir in the cornflour mixture. Simmer gently until it forms a thick custard. Mix together the egg yolks and sugar and stir into the custard. Bring back to the boil, whisking until just bubbling. Remove from the heat. Allow to cool a little, then pour into the pastry case. Spread the mixture evenly.

4 Make the meringue: whisk the egg whites in a large bowl with an electric whisk on full speed until they form stiff peaks. Whisk in the caster sugar, a teaspoon at a time, whisking well and at high speed between each addition.

5 Spoon the meringue over the lemon filling, spreading it out evenly and swirling it into peaks. Make sure there are no gaps. Bake for 45 minutes or until the meringue is crisp and pale beige on the outside and soft and marshmallowy underneath. Serve warm or cold.

Nutrition notes per serving: *412 calories, Protein 6g, Carbohydrate 68g, Fat 15g, Saturated fat 8g, Fibre 1g, Added sugar 39g, Salt 0.37g.*

TIP

The secret of making successful meringues is simple, providing a few straightforward rules are followed. All equipment must be scrupulously clean and dry. Egg whites will not whisk properly if there are any traces of grease and that includes specks of egg yolk. Add the sugar, a teaspoon at a time, slowly at first, adding it more quickly towards the end. To test, lift the whisk out of the bowl; the egg white sticking to it should stand in stiff peaks.

No-cook Desserts

BRANDY CHOCOLATE CHARLOTTE ✿

This is very rich so the slices are quite small. The loaf shape is easy to serve. You'll need to prepare this a day in advance.

Serves 8

about 20 sponge fingers
(Boudoir biscuits)

3 tbsp brandy

FOR THE MOUSSE

115g/4oz plain chocolate,
broken into pieces

2 eggs

175g/6oz unsalted butter, softened

140g/5oz caster sugar

TO DECORATE

150ml/¼ pint whipping cream

grated chocolate (See Tip)

1   Line a 900g/2lb loaf tin with greaseproof paper. Dip eight to nine Boudoir biscuits, sugar-side down, in the brandy. Arrange, sugar-side down, on the base of the loaf tin.

2   Cut the remaining Boudoir biscuits in half and dip, sugar-side down, in the brandy and stand them, sugar-side out, around the edge of the tin.

3   Make the mousse: place the chocolate pieces in a small bowl over a pan of simmering, not boiling, water and allow to melt slowly.

4   Place the melted chocolate, eggs, butter and sugar in a food processor and blend until smooth. Alternatively, cream the butter and sugar, add the chocolate and egg yolks and fold in the beaten egg whites. Turn into the loaf tin and smooth the top, then cover. Chill overnight.

5   The next day, turn out on to a serving dish. Whisk the cream until thick, then pipe rosettes on the Charlotte and sprinkle with grated chocolate.

Nutrition notes per serving: *549 calories, Protein 5g, Carbohydrate 45g, Fat 39g, Saturated fat 22g, Fibre trace, Added sugar 37g, Salt 0.31g.*

✿ *This dessert is best frozen in its tin. Defrost in the fridge for about 8 hours before turning out and decorating.*

TIP

If your chocolate is warm, chill it before grating. Hold the bar in greaseproof paper if you find it becomes sticky.

CAUTION! This recipe contains raw eggs.

GINGER CREAM ROLL

Couldn't be simpler – a real cheat! However, it does need to be made the day before serving.

Serves 4–6

425ml/¾ pint whipping cream

225g/8oz ginger biscuits

4 tbsp brandy

stem ginger slices, to decorate

1   Place half the whipping cream in a bowl and whisk until it forms fairly stiff peaks. Quickly dip each biscuit in a little brandy, then sandwich together with the cream shaping into a long roll. Place on a serving dish, cover and leave in the fridge overnight.

2   The next day, whip the remaining cream and use it to cover the roll completely and to pipe rosettes down the length of the roll. Decorate with slices of stem ginger. To serve, cut the roll in diagonal slices.

Nutrition notes per serving for four: *692 calories, Protein 5g, Carbohydrate 49g, Fat 50g, Saturated fat 30g, Fibre 1g, Added sugar 21g, Salt 0.58g.*

PASSION SPONGE

A variation of my ever-popular passion pudding. It takes all of five minutes to make.

Serves 4–6

18–20cm/7–8in sponge flan case

400g can raspberries in natural juice, drained and juice reserved

a little framboise or cassis liqueur (optional)

150ml/¼ pint double cream

225g/8oz Greek yogurt

1–2 tbsp light muscovado sugar

1   Place the sponge case on a serving plate, then evenly spoon over the raspberries. Sprinkle over a little of the reserved juice with a splash of liqueur, if using.

2   Whisk the double cream until stiff, then fold in the yogurt. Pile on top of the raspberries. Sprinkle over the sugar and chill until the sugar has melted into the topping.

Nutrition notes per serving for four: *508 calories, Protein 10g, Carbohydrate 60g, Fat 27g, Saturated fat 15g, Fibre 2g, Added sugar 42g, Salt 0.25g.*

TIP

If you haven't got a sponge flan-case, place the drained raspberries in a serving dish or individual ramekins, sprinkle over a little juice and liqueur, if using and top with the cream and yogurt mixture. Sprinkle with sugar and chill until it has melted into the topping, then serve sprinkled with a little more sugar.

PINEAPPLE AND GINGER YOGURT FOOL

This is simplicity itself. Serve in attractive glasses or a large serving dish.

Serves 4

14oz can crushed pineapple, drained

4 pieces stem ginger, drained and chopped

425ml/¾ pint Greek-style yogurt

toasted flaked almonds, to serve

1   Mix together the pineapple, stem ginger and Greek-style yogurt.
2   Pour into glasses or a large bowl and chill thoroughly before serving, sprinkled with the almonds.

Nutrition notes per serving: *173 calories, Protein 8g, Carbohydrate 12g, Fat 11g, Saturated fat 6g, Fibre 1g, Added sugar 2g, Salt 0.20g.*

CHOCOLATE TERRINE ✳

Make this the day before you need it as it does need to be chilled overnight in the fridge. Serve very cold, even half frozen, and in very thin slices.

Serves 8–10

225g/8oz milk or plain chocolate, broken into pieces

225g/8oz hard margarine

2 eggs

25g/1oz caster sugar

225g/8oz Nice biscuits

150ml/¼ pint double cream, whipped

chocolate buttons or Maltesers, to decorate

1   Line a 450g/1lb loaf tin with plastic film. Place the chocolate in a pan with the margarine and heat gently until melted. Beat the eggs and sugar together until blended, then gradually add the chocolate mixture a little at a time.
2   Break the biscuits into 1cm/½in pieces and stir into the chocolate mixture. Pack the mixture into the tin and smooth the top. Cover and leave to set in the fridge overnight.
3   Turn out on to a serving dish and peel off the plastic film. Decorate with the whipped cream and chocolate buttons or Maltesers.

Nutrition notes per serving for eight: *610 calories, Protein 6g, Carbohydrate 43g, Fat 47g, Saturated fat 24g, Fibre 1g, Added sugar 24g, Salt 1.02g.*

✳ *Freeze this dessert in its tin. Defrost in the fridge for about 8 hours before turning out and decorating.*

TIP

If your terrine is reluctant to leave the tin, dip the base of the tin briefly in a bowl of hot water, then invert on to a serving plate. Alternatively, wrap the sides and base in a hot damp tea towel for a few moments before turning out.

CAUTION! This recipe contains raw eggs.

LEMON CREAM SYLLABUB

This is a quick creamy pudding made in an electric blender. It is very rich and is best eaten the day it is made.

Serves 4

juice of 2 large lemons

55g/2oz caster sugar

225g/8oz low fat cream cheese

150ml/¼ pint double cream

4 fresh lemon slices and a few pistachio nuts, to decorate

1 Place the lemon juice, sugar and cheese in a blender and blend well. Pour in the double cream and blend until just mixed. Divide the mixture between four individual glasses and chill for several hours.

2 Just before serving, decorate with a twisted slice of lemon and a sprinkling of pistachio nuts.

Nutrition notes per serving: *316 calories, Protein 8g, Carbohydrate 17g, Fat 24g, Saturated fat 14g, Fibre trace, Added sugar 14g, Salt 0.68g.*

FRESH FRUIT SALAD

No desserts book would be complete without a recipe for fruit salad and this one is really delicious as it uses all fresh fruit.

Serves 6

1 Charentais melon

55g/2oz caster sugar

2 thin-skinned oranges, segmented (See Tip)

1 pink grapefruit, segmented (See Tip)

1 small ripe pineapple

1 ripe mango

115g/4oz seedless red or green grapes, strawberries or raspberries

1 Halve the melon and scoop out the seeds with a spoon, then cut into six to eight wedges. Remove the rind and cut the flesh into large chunks. Place in a serving dish and sprinkle with a little of the sugar. Add the orange and grapefruit segments and sprinkle with a little more of the sugar.

2 Top and tail the pineapple. Sit it on its cut base, then cut away the rind in strips, working from the top to the bottom. Quarter the pineapple lengthways and then trim away the central woody core. Slice the pineapple across into chunks and add to the serving dish. Sprinkle with the remaining sugar.

3 Prepare the mango by cutting off thick slices above and below the stone. Trim away the band of flesh around the stone and remove the skin. Cut the flesh from the slices, divide into neat chunks and add to the serving dish. Cover and chill for at least 2 hours. It can be left overnight. Add the grapes, raspberries or strawberries just before serving.

Nutrition notes per serving: *137 calories, Protein 2g, Carbohydrate 34g, Fat 0.5g, Saturated fat none, Fibre 4g, Added sugar 10g, Salt 0.03g.*

TIP

To make orange and grapefruit segments: peel the fruit, slice off the top and bottom, then standing the fruit on one cut end cut the pith and peel off in strips, exposing the flesh. Holding each fruit over the bowl to catch the juices, cut in between the membranes to release each segment.

Soufflés

HOT LEMON SOUFFLÉ PUDDING

This is one of my favourite lemon puddings. I have even, for one reason or another, baked it ahead of time and reheated it very satisfactorily in a roasting tin of water for 30 minutes in a moderate oven. The top of the pudding is a spongy mousse while underneath is a sharp lemon sauce.

Serves 4–6

85g/3oz soft baking margarine, plus extra for greasing

250g/9oz caster sugar

3 eggs, separated

85g/3oz self-raising flour

grated rind and juice of 2 lemons

425ml/¾ pint milk

1 Preheat the oven to 375F/190C/Gas 5. Grease a shallow 1.4 litre/2½ pint ovenproof dish.

2 Place the margarine and caster sugar in a bowl and beat until smooth. Beat in the egg yolks, then beat in the flour, lemon rind, juice and milk. Do not worry if the mixture looks curdled at this stage – it is quite normal. Alternatively, place the egg yolks, lemon rind and juice, margarine, sugar and flour into a food processor and blend well, then add the milk through the funnel with the machine running.

3 Whisk the egg whites until they form soft peaks, then carefully fold them into the lemon mixture using a large metal spoon.

4 Pour the mixture into the ovenproof dish and place in a roasting tin. Pour in enough boiling water to come halfway up the dish and bake for 1 hour or until pale golden brown on top.

Nutrition notes per serving for four: *600 calories, Protein 10g, Carbohydrate 87g, Fat 26g, Saturated fat 7g, Fibre 1g, Added sugar 66g, Salt 0.91g.*

TIP

Buy thin-skinned lemons that feel heavy for their size. To get maximum juice from them, it helps if the fruit is warm, or at least at room temperature. If you have a microwave, cut the fruit in half, place cut side down on a plate and microwave on high for a few seconds. When grating the rind, wash and dry the fruit well. Grate the rind on the small-holed side of the grater, making sure you scrape everything off the back of the grater. A pastry brush is a useful tool for this tricky job.

HOT CHOCOLATE SOUFFLÉ

If you can make a white sauce you can make a hot soufflé. Soufflés are not difficult but need a bit of care with the timing. It is essential to use the correct sized soufflé dish so that the soufflé rises above it. Measure the soufflé dish that you have by pouring measured water in it to give you the capacity. I then write the size on the bottom of the dish with a waterproof marker pen to remind me next time. If you are serving a soufflé for a supper party make the sauce base ahead of time, including the addition of the yolks and flavouring, then 40 minutes before baking and serving fold in the whisked egg whites, turn into the dish and bake.

Serves 4

115g/4oz plain chocolate, broken into pieces

300ml/½ pint milk

40g/1½oz butter, plus extra for greasing

40g/1½oz plain flour

¼ tsp vanilla extract

4 large eggs, separated

55g/2oz caster sugar

sifted icing sugar, for dusting

whipped cream, to serve

1 Preheat the oven to 375F/190C/Gas 5 and place a baking sheet in it. Butter a 1.2 litre/2 pint soufflé dish.

2 Place the chocolate, two tablespoons of water and two tablespoons of milk in a pan. Stir over a low heat until the chocolate has melted, then add the remaining milk and bring to the boil. Remove the pan from the heat.

3 Melt the butter in a small pan, stir in the flour and cook for 2 minutes without browning. Remove from the heat and stir in the hot milk, return to the heat and bring to the boil, stirring until thickened. Add the vanilla extract and leave to cool.

4 Beat the egg yolks, one at a time, into the chocolate sauce, then sprinkle over the sugar. Whisk the egg whites until they are stiff but not dry. Stir one tablespoon into the mixture, then carefully fold in the remainder.

5 Pour into the soufflé dish, run a teaspoon round the edge and bake on the hot baking tray in the centre of the oven for about 40 minutes. Sprinkle with icing sugar and serve at once with whipped cream.

Nutrition notes per serving: *449 calories, Protein 12g, Carbohydrate46g, Fat 26g, Saturated fat 14g, Fibre trace, Added sugar 33g, Salt 0.50g.*

TIP

For an orange soufflé, add the finely grated rind of two small oranges and the juice of half an orange to the mixture, instead of the chocolate and two tablespoons of water. Omit the vanilla extract and increase the caster sugar to 85g/3oz. For a coffee soufflé, add two tablespoons of coffee essence to the milk and omit the vanilla extract.

Favourite Hot Puds

CLASSIC APPLE PIE ✿

This is always supposed to be a great favourite with men. I must say that, well made, there is really nothing to beat it. I know that it is not correct but I always decorate my sweet pies with lots of pastry leaves, they look more inviting. Serve with my Basic ice cream (see page 62).

Serves 4–6

675g/1½lb cooking apples, peeled, cored and cut into thick slices

55–85g/2–3oz caster sugar

4 whole cloves

FOR THE PASTRY

175g/6oz plain flour

40g/1½oz hard margarine, cubed

40g/1½oz white vegetable fat, cubed

milk, to glaze

granulated sugar, for sprinkling

1 Use an 850ml/1½ pint shallow pie dish. Arrange half the apples in the bottom of the dish, sprinkle with the caster sugar and arrange the cloves evenly among the apples. Cover with the remaining apple slices and add three tablespoons of cold water.

2 Make the pastry: place the flour in a bowl, add the fats and rub in with your fingertips until the mixture resembles fine breadcrumbs. Add sufficient cold water (about two tablespoons) to mix to a firm dough.

3 Roll out the pastry on a lightly floured work surface and cover the top of the pie dish. Use any pastry trimmings to decorate, if liked. Chill for 30 minutes.

4 Preheat the oven to 400F/200C/Gas 6. Brush the pie with a little milk, then sprinkle the top with sugar. Make a small slit in the centre of the pie for the steam to escape and bake for about 40–45 minutes until the apples are tender and the pastry is crisp and pale golden. Cover if the pastry starts to brown before the apples are cooked.

Nutrition notes per serving for four: *416 calories, Protein 5g, Carbohydrate 61g, Fat 19g, Saturated fat 7g, Fibre 3g, Added sugar 16g, Salt 0.21g.*

✿ *Freeze the pie after cooking and when cool. Leave to defrost almost completely before reheating and serving. Uncooked home-made pastry is an excellent stand-by for the freezer. Pack in separate quantities of 225g/8oz and 450g/1lb, labelling clearly. Defrost in the fridge or kitchen until pliable enough to roll and use.*

TIP

For perfect pastry every time, make sure your hands are cold (run them under the cold tap, if needs be), use cold, preferably iced, water and roll out on a cool surface – marble is best. Chilling the pastry for 30 minutes before baking prevents it shrinking as it cooks.

APPLE AND MINCEMEAT STEAMED PUDDING

The breadcrumbs give this pudding an extra-light texture.

175g/6oz self-raising flour

55g/2oz fresh white breadcrumbs

115g/4oz shredded beef or vegetarian suet

150ml/¼ pint milk

225g/8oz mincemeat

450g/1lb cooking apples, peeled, cored and sliced

55g/2oz light muscovado sugar

custard, to serve

1   Butter a 1.2 litre/2 pint pudding basin. Place the flour, breadcrumbs and suet in a bowl. Add sufficient milk to make a soft dough and divide into three portions, in graded sizes.

2   Roll out the smallest portion to line the base of the basin. Add half the mincemeat, apples and sugar, then roll out the second portion of pastry to fit over the fruit. Place the remaining fruit on top, then cover with the remaining pastry rolled out to fit the basin.

3   Cover with a greased and pleated lid of greaseproof paper and a lid of foil. Steam in a steamer, or place in a large pan with enough boiling water to come halfway up the basin for about 3 hours (see Tip). Turn out and serve with custard.

Nutrition notes per serving: *462 calories, Protein 5g, Carbohydrate 70g, Fat 20g, Saturated fat 9g, Fibre 3g, Added sugar 15g, Salt 0.62g.*

TIP

Keep the water boiling in the pan, topping up when needed with more boiling water. Stand the basin on an old, upturned saucer to keep it off the pan bottom.

TREACLE SPONGES

A great family favourite for a cold winter's day.

Serves 4

4 tbsp golden syrup

1 tbsp fresh lemon juice

grated rind of 1 lemon

115g/4oz soft margarine

115g/4oz caster sugar

2 eggs

115g/4oz self-raising flour

1 tsp baking powder

warm golden syrup, to serve

1   Grease four 175ml/6fl oz pudding basins. Blend the syrup with the lemon juice and divide between the basins.

2   Place all the remaining ingredients in a bowl and beat well for 2 minutes or until well blended. Divide the mixture between the basins and smooth the tops. Cover each basin with a greased and pleated lid of greaseproof paper and foil.

3   Steam in a steamer, or place in a large pan with enough boiling water to come halfway up each basin for 45 minutes (See Tip, above). Turn out and serve with extra, warm golden syrup.

Nutrition notes per serving: *519 calories, Protein 6g, Carbohydrate 69g, Fat 27g, Saturated fat 5g, Fibre 2g, Added sugar 46g, Salt 1.45g.*

STICKY APRICOT PUDDING

This is a very adaptable recipe and one of my family's favouries. It is good if you are in a hurry, for instance if you have forgotten to make a pudding for Sunday lunch. You will probably have all the ingredients in the pantry and you can use a variety of different fruits, either fresh or canned (See Tip). Just place the pudding on the top shelf, above the roast, and let it cook there. It couldn't be easier.

Serves 6–8

175g/6oz self-raising flour

1 tsp baking powder

55g/2oz caster sugar

55g/2oz soft margarine

1 egg

grated rind of 1 lemon

150ml/¼ pint milk

2 x 410g cans apricot halves, drained

FOR THE TOPPING

55g/2oz butter, melted

175g/6oz demerara sugar

1 Preheat the oven to 450F/230C/Gas 8. Grease a shallow 28cm/11in ovenproof baking dish.

2 Place the flour, baking powder, sugar, margarine, egg, lemon rind and milk in a bowl. Beat together until the mixture foms a soft, cake-like consistency.

3 Spread the mixture over the base of the dish and arrange the apricots, cut-side down, over the top. Brush or drizzle the butter over the apricots, then sprinkle with the demerara sugar.

4 Bake for 35 minutes or until the top has caramelised to a deep golden brown. Serve warm with crème fraîche, whipped cream, ice cream or even hot custard on a cold winter day.

Nutrition notes per serving: *443 calories, Protein 5g, Carbohydrate 71g, Fat 17g, Saturated fat 7g, Fibre 2g, Added sugar 40g, Salt 0.96g.*

TIP

You can substitute many other fruits, whatever you have to hand. Both sliced dessert and cooking apples work well, try the delicious English Bramley. If you have an apple tree, this is a good way to use the windfalls. Arrange the slices evenly over the top of the sponge mixture. Other good alternatives are rhubarb or plums. Cut the plums in half and remove the stones, then arrange them cut side down. You can really let your imagination run riot, choosing unusual fruits or even a combination of fruits which will complement each other.

Chilled Desserts

EASY LEMON CHEESECAKE ✳

The cheesecake originated long ago in Russia and Eastern Europe, and consisted of the local soft cheese, some sugar and eggs baked in a pastry case. I suppose at one time it was a traditional and delicious means of using up eggs and a little bit of cheese. Cooked cheesecakes are a speciality of countries like Austria, Germany and France, although there is a long tradition in Britain, too, dating from at least the 13th century. This is a real cheat but so delicious. You can also make this in a loose-bottomed cake tin.

Serves 6

FOR THE BASE

10 digestive biscuits, crushed

55g/2oz butter, melted

25g/1oz demerara sugar

FOR THE FILLING

150ml/¼ pint double cream

400g can condensed milk (See Tip)

115g/4oz low-fat soft cheese, softened

grated rind and juice of 3 large lemons

FOR THE TOPPING

150ml/¼ pint whipping cream, whipped

fresh strawberries or grapes, to decorate

1 Mix together the crushed biscuits, butter and demerara sugar to make the biscuit base. Turn into a 20cm/8in spring-release tin or fluted china flan dish and using a metal spoon, press evenly over the base and sides. Leave to set.

2 Make the filling: in a bowl, mix together the cream, condensed milk, soft cheese and lemon rind, then add the lemon juice a little at a time, whisking until the mixture thickens. Pour into the flan case and leave to chill, covered, in the fridge for 3–4 hours or overnight.

3 Decorate with swirls of whipped cream and fresh strawberries or grapes.

Nutrition notes per serving: *611 calories, Protein 11g, Carbohydrate 64g, Fat 36g, Saturated fat 21g, Fibre 1g, Added sugar 39g, Salt 1.12g.*

✳ *Open freeze, then cover with foil if still in its container or place in a rigid plastic box to protect it. Defrost in the fridge before decorating with whipped cream and fresh fruit.*

TIP

Condensed milk is used as a sweetener in some recipes. It is canned milk from which half the water content has been removed, and to which sugar has been added. (It makes wonderful toffee and fudge.)

CRÈME BRÛLÉE

This is sheer luxury, and is not difficult to make. Choose a shallow dish that will withstand being put under the grill. Make the cream custard part a day ahead, then put the sugar topping on and caramelise it about three hours before serving. This is a very good way of using up surplus egg yolks and the single cream gives it a modern twist. Use the whites for making a meringue dessert (pages 10–17).

Serves 6–8

4 egg yolks

25g/1oz caster sugar and a few drops of vanilla extract or vanilla sugar (See Tip)

600ml/1 pint single cream

about 55g/2oz demerara sugar

1 Preheat the oven to 325F/160C/Gas 3. Thoroughly butter a shallow 850ml/1½ pint ovenproof dish or six to eight small ramekins.

2 Beat the egg yolks with the caster sugar and few drops of vanilla extract or the vanilla sugar. Heat the cream to scalding, just too hot to put your finger in! Leave to cool slightly, then beat into the egg yolks, beating all the time. Pour into the dish or ramekins.

3 Stand the dish in a roasting tin half-filled with hot water and bake the custard for 45 minutes or until set. If using ramekins, they will only need 25–30 minutes cooking time. Remove from the oven and cool. Cover, then chill in the fridge overnight. These can be made 2 days ahead.

4 Preheat the grill to hot. Sprinkle the top of the custard with demerara sugar to about 5mm/¼in thickness and place under the grill, near the top, until the sugar melts, then caramelises to a golden brown. This takes 3–4 minutes. Keep a careful watch to make sure the sugar does not burn. Chill for 2–3 hours before serving. Chilling again after caramelising the sugar gives time for the hard topping to become slightly less hard, easier to crack and serve. If you leave it considerably longer, the caramel will melt and soften which is not nearly so attractive and does not taste as good.

Nutrition notes per serving for six: *291 calories, Protein 5g, Carbohydrate 18g, Fat 23g, Saturated fat 13g, Fibre none, Added sugar 14g, Salt 0.14g.*

TIP

Vanilla sugar adds a wonderful flavour. Simply store two or three vanilla pods in a jar of caster sugar. After about two weeks, the sugar is imbued with the pungency of the vanilla. As you use the sugar, just top up the jar with more.

CONTINENTAL CHEESECAKE

This is a traditional cooked cheesecake. Expect the sides of the cake to be a little higher than the centre after baking – it gives a nice dip to take the blackcurrant or cherry topping.

Serves 10

FOR THE BASE

85g/3oz digestive biscuits, crushed

40g/1½oz butter, melted

25g/1oz demerara sugar

FOR THE FILLING

55g/2oz soft margarine

175g/6oz caster sugar

450g/1lb curd cheese

25g/1oz plain flour

finely grated rind and juice
of 1 lemon

3 eggs, separated

150ml/¼ pint double cream,
lightly whipped

FOR THE TOPPING

425g can blackcurrants or pitted
black cherries

1 heaped tsp arrowroot

a little kirsch (optional)

150ml/¼ pint double cream,
whipped, to decorate

1   Preheat the oven to 325F/160C/Gas 3. Lightly oil a 23cm/9in spring-release or loose-bottomed cake tin, then line the base and sides with greaseproof paper.

2   Make the base: mix together the biscuits, butter and sugar and spread over the base of the tin. Press down firmly with the back of a metal spoon. Leave to set.

3   Make the filling: place the margarine, sugar, curd cheese, flour, lemon rind and juice and the egg yolks in a large bowl. Beat until smooth. Fold in the cream. Whisk the egg whites until stiff, then fold into the mixture. Pour on to the biscuit crust.

4   Bake for 1 hour or until set. Turn off the oven and leave the cheesecake in the oven for a further 1 hour to cool. Run a knife round the edge of the tin to loosen the cheesecake, then release the spring clip or push the base up through the cake tin. Remove the side and base papers.

5   Make the topping: place the fruit with its juice in a small pan. Dissolve the arrowroot in a little cold water and mix into the fruit. Bring up to the boil to thicken the juice, adding a dash of kirsch for flavour, if using. Allow to cool completely, then pile on top of the cheesecake.

6   Decorate the edge of the cheesecake with piped or spooned whipped double cream.

Nutrition notes per serving: *451 calories, Protein 10g, Carbohydrate 35g, Fat 31g, Saturated fat 16g, Fibre 2g, Added sugar 22g, Salt 0.91g.*

TIP

You can subsitute fresh fruit – strawberries, raspberries, red and blackcurrants and blackberries – for the topping when in season. Simply cook red and blackcurrants in two tablespoons of water and sweeten to taste. Add the softer fruits to the cooled thickened syrup. Alternatively, frozen mixed summer fruits are available throughout the year from supermarkets. Defrost, place in the pan with their juices, adding a little cold water if there is not enough liquid, then add the dissolved arrowroot.

CRÈME CARAMEL

The secret of making Crème caramel is to cook it slowly so that the custard does not boil and make the crème tough and full of holes. Serve Crème caramel very cold. Leave in the soufflé dish or ramekins until the very last moment before turning out, or you will find that the caramel topping loses its shine and colour.

Serves 6

FOR THE CARAMEL
115g/4oz granulated sugar
FOR THE CREME
6 eggs
55g/2oz caster sugar
few drops vanilla essence
700ml/1¼ pints milk

1 Preheat the oven to 300F/150C/Gas 2. Make the caramel: place the sugar and three tablespoons of water in a heavy-based pan and dissolve the sugar, stirring occasionally, over a low heat. When the sugar has dissolved, bring to the boil, without stirring, and boil rapidly until the syrup is a pale golden brown. Remove from the heat and quickly pour the caramel into six small ramekins or a 1 litre/1¾ pint soufflé dish.

2 Make the crème: mix together the eggs, sugar and vanilla essence. Warm the milk in a pan over a low heat until it is hand-hot, then pour it on to the egg mixture, stirring constantly.

3 Butter the sides of the ramekins or dish above the caramel. Strain the crème through a fine sieve, into the ramekins or dish and place in a roasting tin half-filled with hot water.

4 Bake the crème in the ramekins for about 45 minutes or in the soufflé dish for about 1 hour or until a knife inserted in the centre comes out clean. Do not worry if it takes longer than the time given to cook. It will set eventually. Do not increase the oven temperature or the crème will have bubbles in it.

5 Remove from the oven and leave to cool completely for at least 12 hours or overnight in the fridge. Turn out carefully on to a flat dish or dishes sufficiently deep to catch the caramel juices.

Nutrition notes per serving: *320 calories, Protein 16g, Carbohydrate 31g, Fat 15g, Saturated fat 6g, Fibre none, Added sugar 25g, Salt 0.52g.*

TIP

Do not attempt to make caramel in a pan that is non-stick or has a dark interior. You cannot see clearly when the caramel is dark enough, and I have found it impossible to make a caramel in a non-stick pan. The syrup crystallises and will not caramelise. Heavy-gauge aluminium or stainless steel pans are best.

BUTTERMILK AND HONEY CHEESECAKE

This is a lovely, subtly flavoured cooked cheesecake.

Serves 8

20cm/8in sponge flan case

1 tbsp clear honey, to glaze

FOR THE FILLING

225g/8oz full-fat soft cheese

3 eggs, separated

85g/3oz caster sugar

2 rounded tbsp clear honey

55g/2oz ground almonds

1 tsp almond essence

40g/1½oz plain flour

300ml/½ pint buttermilk

handful flaked almonds

1 Preheat the oven to 325F/160C/Gas 3. Lightly grease a 20cm/8in loose-bottomed cake tin or spring-release tin. Slip the sponge flan case into the tin, trimming to fit if necessary.

2 Place the cheese in a large bowl and beat until soft. Beat in the egg yolks with 25g/1oz of the sugar, the honey, ground almonds, almond essence, flour and the buttermilk.

3 In a separate bowl, whisk the egg whites until stiff, then whisk in the remaining caster sugar. Fold into the cheese mixture, then spoon the mixture on top of the sponge and sprinkle with the flaked almonds.

4 Bake for 1¼ hours or until firm but still spongy to the touch. Turn off the oven, open the door and leave the cheesecake to cool inside.

5 Ease the cheesecake away from the sides of the tin with a small palette knife and slide on to a serving plate. Gently heat the honey in a small pan and brush over the top of the cheesecake to glaze.

Nutrition notes per serving: *338 calories, Protein 11g, Carbohydrate 37g, Fat 17g, Saturated fat 1g, Fibre 1g, Added sugar 26g, Salt 0.41g.*

ORANGE JAFFA CHEESECAKE

A very smooth, fresh cheesecake, the ginger biscuits go well with the orange. A family favourite.

Serves 8

FOR THE BASE

115g/4oz ginger biscuits, crushed

55g/2oz butter, melted

25g/1oz demerara sugar

FOR THE FILLING

600ml/1 pint packet orange jelly

150ml/¼ pint Jaffa orange juice

juice of 2 lemons

350g/12oz full-fat cream cheese

115g/4oz caster sugar

150ml/¼ pint whipping cream, whipped

small can mandarin oranges, drained

1 Lightly grease a 20cm/8in round loose-bottomed cake tin or spring-release tin. Start to make the cheesecake: dissolve the jelly in 150ml/¼ pint of boiling water, then add the orange and lemon juice. Leave in a cold place until the jelly is thick and nearly set. (This will take about 30 minutes.)

2 Meanwhile, mix together the base ingredients and spread over the base of the tin, pressing down firmly.

3 Mix the cream cheese with the sugar and the almost set jelly, then fold in the whipped cream. Spoon into the tin and leave to set, covered, in a cool place.

4 To serve, loosen the sides of the cheesecake from the tin and push up the base and slide on to a plate. Or release the spring clip. Arrange the mandarin oranges around the edge of the cheesecake. You could decorate this with fresh mint sprigs for added freshness.

Nutrition notes per serving: *503 calories, Protein 4g, Carbohydrate 44g, Fat 36g, Saturated fat 22g, Fibre trace, Added sugar 34g, Salt 0.63g.*

Chocolate Desserts

CHOCOLATE ROULADE ✸

Don't worry that the sponge cracks as it is rolled – it is meant to and is part of its charm. Make it the day before, or in the morning ready for the meal in the evening.

Serves 6–8

175g/6oz plain chocolate, broken into pieces

6 eggs, size 2, separated

175g/6oz caster sugar

TO DECORATE

sifted icing sugar, for dusting

300ml/½ pint double cream, whipped

1 Preheat the oven to 350F/180C/Gas 4. Grease a 33x23cm/13x9in Swiss roll tin and line with greased greaseproof or non-stick baking paper.

2 Place the chocolate in a bowl over a pan of hand-hot water. Allow the chocolate to gently melt. Cool slightly.

3 Place the egg yolks and sugar in a large bowl and with an electric whisk, whisk on full speed until light and creamy. Carefully stir in the melted chocolate until evenly blended.

4 Whisk the egg whites until stiff but not dry, then fold gently into the chocolate mixture. Turn into the tin and gently ease the mixture into the corners. Level the surface and bake for 20 minutes or until firm to the touch.

5 Remove from the oven and, while still hot, place a dry tea towel gently down on top of the cake while still in the tin. Place another tea towel, soaked with water and wrung out, on top (See Tip). Leave in a cool place overnight.

6 Remove the tea towels and invert the cake on to a piece of greasepoof paper which has been liberally sprinkled with icing sugar. Remove the paper lining and spread the cake with whipped cream. Roll up the roulade from the long edge using the paper to help, and dust with more icing sugar, to decorate. If you prefer a fat roulade, roll it from the short edge.

Nutrition notes per serving for six: *580 calories, Protein 9g, Carbohydrate 53g, Fat 38g, Saturated fat 22g, Fibre none, Added sugar 50g, Salt 0.25g.*

✸ *Open freeze the filled roulade, then cover with foil. Defrost in the fridge for about 8 hours before dusting with more icing sugar. If you have any left over, cut into wedges, wrap individually and freeze. These will defrost in 30 minutes.*

TIP

This cake must be kept damp before rolling. Instead of covering with two tea towels, place a cooling rack over the top of the cake in the tin. Place a damp tea towel on top of the rack, and place the whole lot in a large plastic bag and leave for several hours or overnight.

DEATH BY CHOCOLATE CAKE

A moist chocolate cake that really can't go wrong and keeps well.

Serves 8–10

190g/6½oz plain flour

2 tbsp cocoa (See Tip)

1 tsp bicarbonate of soda

1 tsp baking powder

140g/5oz caster sugar

2 tbsp golden syrup

2 eggs, beaten

150ml/¼ pint sunflower oil

150ml/¼ pint milk

FOR THE ICING AND FILLING

3 tbsp apricot jam

140g/5oz plain chocolate, broken into pieces

150ml/¼ pint double cream

1   Preheat the oven to 325F/160C/Gas 3. Grease and base line two 20cm/8in straight-sided sandwich tins with greased greaseproof paper.

2   Sift the dry ingredients into a large bowl and make a well in the centre. Add the syrup, eggs, oil and milk and beat well. Divide between the tins, then bake for 30-35 minutes or until the cake springs back when lightly pressed with the fingertips. Turn out on to a wire rack, remove the paper and leave to cool.

3   Warm the apricot jam in a small pan, then spread a little over the base of one cake and the top of the other.

4   Combine the chocolate and cream in a pan and heat over a gentle heat until the chocolate has melted and the cream is hot. Remove from the heat and stir the mixture to ensure it is fully melted and smooth. Leave to cool until on the point of setting, then spread on top of the apricot jam on both cakes.

5   Stack the top cake on the base one and use a small palette knife to decorate the top, drawing 'S' shapes from the centre to give a swirled effect. Keep in a cool place until ready to serve.

Nutrition notes per serving for eight: *528 calories, Protein 6g, Carbohydrate 59g, Fat 31g, Saturated fat 12g, Fibre 1g, Added sugar 38g, Salt 0.84g.*

TIP

Cocoa powder is pure chocolate liquor from which much of the cocoa butter has been extracted. It is then ground into a fine powder. This undoubtedly gives the most inexpensive, strongest and best chocolate flavour in baking. Don't be tempted to substitute with drinking chocolate powder, as the added sugar in drinking chocolate will give a very mild, sweet flavour to the cake.

PROFITEROLES AND CHOCOLATE ECLAIRS ✷

Choux pastry must be well cooked until really firm and a good straw colour. The profiteroles look wonderful piled up in a pyramid.

Makes about 12 eclairs or 20 profiteroles

FOR THE CHOUX PASTRY

55g/2oz hard margarine or butter

70g/2½oz plain flour, sifted

2 eggs, beaten

FOR THE FILLING

300ml/½ pint whipping cream, whipped

FOR THE ICING

55g/2oz plain chocolate, broken into pieces

15g/½oz butter

85g/3oz icing sugar, sifted

1   Preheat the oven to 425F/220C/Gas 7. Lightly grease two baking sheets.

2   Make the pastry: place the margarine and 150ml/¼ pint water in a small pan. Allow the fat to melt, then bring slowly to the boil. Remove the pan from the heat, add the flour all at once and beat until the mixture forms a soft ball. Beat over the heat for a further 1 minute. Cool slightly, then gradually beat in the eggs, beating well between each addition, to give a smooth shiny paste.

3   Spoon the mixture into a piping bag fitted with a 1cm/½in plain nozzle and either pipe small mounds for the profiteroles or 12, 13–15cm/5–6in long eclair shapes, leaving room for them to spread.

4   Bake for 10 minutes, then reduce the oven temperature to 375F/190C/Gas 5. Cook the profiteroles for a further 10 minutes, the eclairs for 20 minutes or until well risen, and a deep golden brown. Remove from the oven and split open to allow the steam to escape. (This keeps the pastry crisp.) If you like the centres really dry, return to the oven after splitting, at 350F/180C/Gas 4 for a further 10 minutes. Cool on a wire rack.

5   Using a piping bag fitted with a plain nozzle, fill each profiterole or eclair with a little of the whipped cream.

6   Make the icing: melt the chocolate in a bowl over a pan of simmering, not boiling, water with two tablespoons of water and the butter. Remove from the heat and beat in the icing sugar until smooth. Dip each profiterole or eclair into the icing to coat the top, then leave to set.

Nutrition notes per serving for 12: *220 calories, Protein 2g, Carbohydrate 16g, Fat 17g, Saturated fat 10g, Fibre trace, Added sugar 10g, Salt 0.17g.*

✷ *The choux pastry can be frozen before cooking or after baking. To freeze uncooked, pipe shapes on to baking sheets lined with freezer film and open freeze. When firm, pack into freezer bags for up to 3 months. Cook from frozen allowing a few extra minutes cooking time. For baked items, split and cool before freezing and pack in rigid plastic containers to protect them from breaking. Keep for 3–6 months. Crisp up defrosted pastries in a hot oven for a minute or two, then cool and fill.*

TIP

Do not fill choux pastry items too long before serving as the pastry tends to go soggy.

Ice Creams

BASIC SPECIAL ICE CREAM

This is the perfect ice cream to make; no need for an ice cream machine.

TV Cooks *MARY BERRY COOKS PUDDINGS AND DESSERTS*

Serves 6–8

4 eggs, separated

115g/4oz caster sugar

300ml/½ pint whipping cream

a few drops vanilla extract (optional)

1 Whisk the egg yolks in a small bowl until blended. In a larger bowl whisk the egg whites with an electric whisk on high speed until they are stiff, then whisk in the sugar still at high speed, a teaspoon at a time. The whites will get stiffer and stiffer as the sugar is added.

2 Whisk the cream until it forms soft peaks, then fold into the meringue mixture with the egg yolks. Add vanilla extract, if using.

3 Turn the mixture into a 1.4 litre/2½ pint container, cover, then place in the freezer overnight. Leave to defrost at room temperature for 5 minutes before serving in scoops in small glasses or dishes.

Nutrition notes per serving for six: *311 calories, Protein 5g, Carbohydrate 22g, Fat 23g, Saturated fat 13g, Fibre none, Added sugar 20g, Salt 0.17g.*

TIP

This special ice cream needs no whisking during freezing.

PINEAPPLE ICE CREAM

This is one of my favourite ice cream flavours.

Serves 6–8

flesh of 1 small pineapple

juice of 1 small lemon

55g/2oz icing sugar

4 eggs, separated

115g/4oz caster sugar

300ml/½ pint double cream

1 Place the pineapple flesh, lemon juice and icing sugar in a blender and purée. Freeze until just set.

2 Make the ice cream: whisk the egg yolks in a small bowl until blended. In a larger bowl whisk the egg whites with an electric whisk on high speed until they are stiff, then whisk in the sugar, a teaspoon at a time. The whites will get stiffer and stiffer as the sugar is added.

3 Whisk the cream until it forms soft peaks, then fold it into the meringue mixture with the egg yolks. Stir in the pineapple purée.

4 Turn the mixture into a 1.4 litre/2½ pint container, cover, then place in the freezer overnight. Leave to defrost at room temperature for 5 minutes before serving in scoops in small glasses or dishes.

Nutrition notes per serving for six: *426 calories, Protein 5g, Carbohydrate 41g, Fat 28g, Saturated fat 16g, Fibre 1g, Added sugar 30g, Salt 0.17g.*

CAUTION! Both these recipes contain raw eggs.

Other Titles in the *TV Cooks* Series

Michael Barry Cooks Crafty Classics
Valentina Harris Cooks Italian
Ken Hom Cooks Chinese
Madhur Jaffrey Cooks Curries
Keith Floyd Cooks Barbecues

Other Titles by Mary Berry available from BBC Books

Mary Berry at Home
Mary Berry's Quick & Easy Cakes
Mary Berry's Ultimate Cake Book

INDEX

Page numbers in bold refer to photographs

Alaska, speedy baked 12, 13

apples 25
- Apple and mincemeat steamed pudding 42, **43**
- Classic apple pie **40**, 41
- Filo apple strudels **20**, 21
- Tarte Tatin **24**, 25

apricots
- Sticky apricot pudding **44**, 45

bananas
- Coffee and banana vacherin 14, **15**

Brandy chocolate charlotte 28, 29

Buttermilk and honey cheesecake 54, **55**

cheesecakes
- Buttermilk and honey cheesecake 54, **55**
- Continental cheesecake 50, **51**
- Easy lemon cheesecake 46, **47**
- Orange jaffa cheesecake 54, **55**

chocolate 22, 58
- Brandy chocolate charlotte **28**, 29
- Chocolate roulade **56**, 57
- Chocolate terrine **32**, 33
- Death by chocolate cake 58, **59**
- Hot chocolate soufflé 38, **39**
- Mississippi mud pie 22, **23**
- Profiteroles and chocolate eclairs **60**, 61

Coffee and banana vacherin 14, 15

condensed milk
- Easy lemon cheesecake 46, **47**

Crème brûlée 48, **49**

Crème caramel 52, 53

Death by chocolate cake 58, 59

eggs
- Chocolate roulade **56**, 57
- Crème brûlée **48**, 49
- Crème caramel **52**, 53
- *see also* ice cream; meringues; soufflés

Filo pastry 21
- Filo apple strudels **20**, 21

fruit
- Continental cheesecake 50, **51**
- Fresh fruit salad 34, **35**
- Pavlova **12**, 13
- Sticky pudding **44**, 45

ginger biscuits
- Ginger cream roll 30, **31**
- Orange jaffa cheesecake 54, **55**

ginger, stem
- Pineapple and ginger yogurt fool **32**, 33

Hazelnut meringue cake 16, 17

honey
- Buttermilk and honey cheesecake 54, **55**

ice cream
- Basic special ice cream 62
- Pineapple ice cream 62
- Speedy baked Alaska **12**, 13

lemon curd
- Lemon cream fruit tarts 18, **19**

lemons 37
- Easy lemon cheesecake 46, **47**
- Hot lemon soufflé pudding **36**, 37
- Lemon cream syllabub 34, **35**
- Lemon meringue pie 26, **27**

meringues 26
- Coffee and banana vacherin 14, **15**
- Hazelnut meringue cake **16**, 17
- Lemon meringue pie 26, **27**
- Pavlova **12**, 13
- Raspberry meringue roulade 10, **11**
- Speedy baked Alaska **12**, 13

mincemeat
- Apple and mincemeat steamed pudding 42, **43**

Mississippi mud pie 22, 23

oranges 34
- Orange jaffa cheesecake 54, **55**
- Speedy baked Alaska **12**, 13

Passion sponge 30, **31**

Pavlova 12, 13

pineapple
- Pineapple and ginger yogurt fool **32**, 33
- Pineapple ice cream 62

Profiteroles and chocolate eclairs 60, 61

raspberries
- Passion sponge 30, **31**
- Raspberry coulis 17
- Raspberry meringue roulade 10, **11**

roulades
- Chocolate roulade **56**, 57
- Raspberry meringue roulade 10, **11**

shortbread
- Lemon cream fruit tarts 18, **19**

soufflés
- Hot chocolate soufflé 38, **39**
- Hot lemon soufflé pudding **36**, 37

strawberries
- Lemon cream fruit tarts 18, **19**

Tarte Tatin 24, 25

Treacle sponges 42, 43

vacherin, Coffee and banana 14, 15

vanilla sugar 49

yogurt
- Pineapple and ginger yogurt fool **32**, 33